What Can I Be?

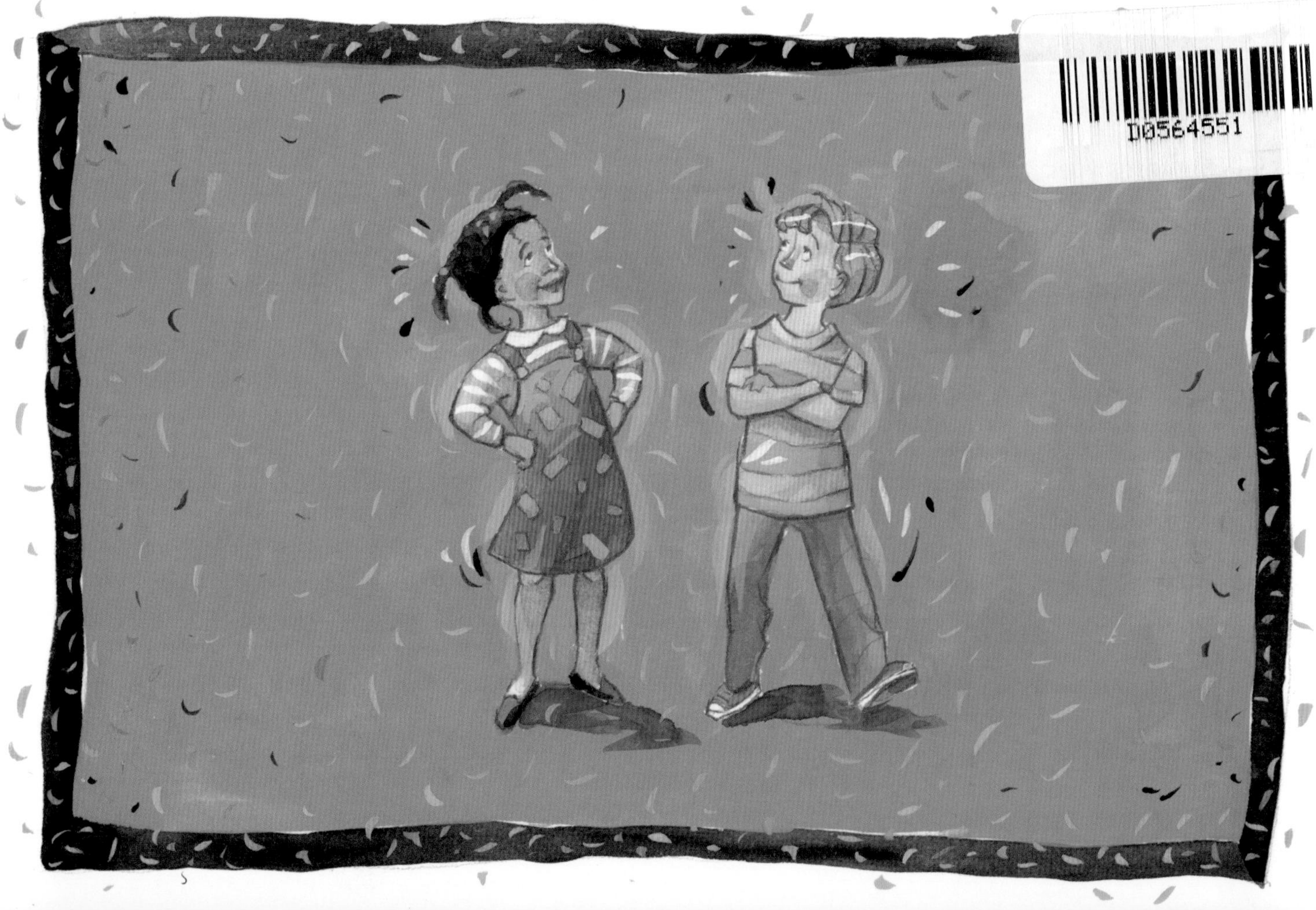

D0564551

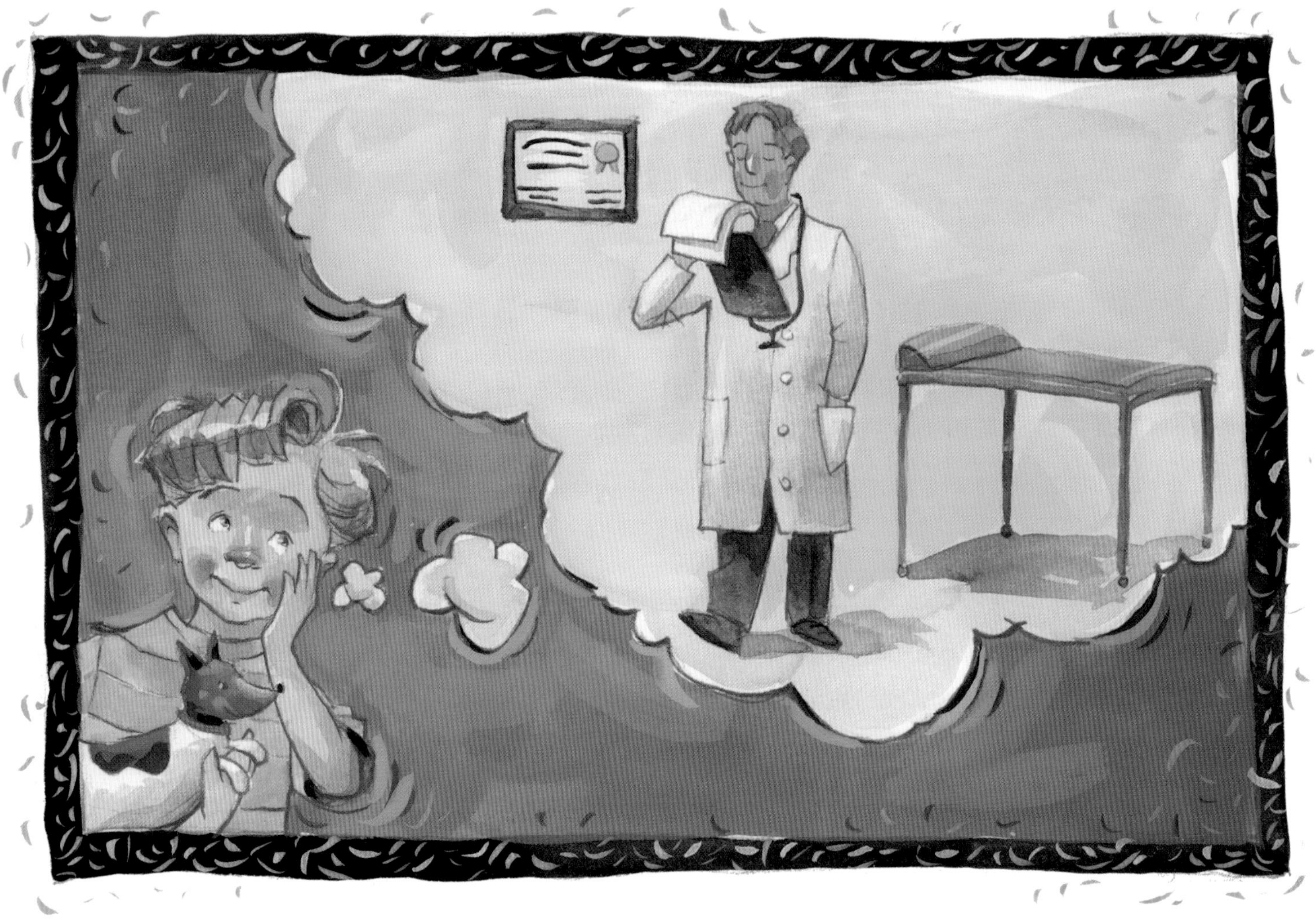

I can be a doctor.

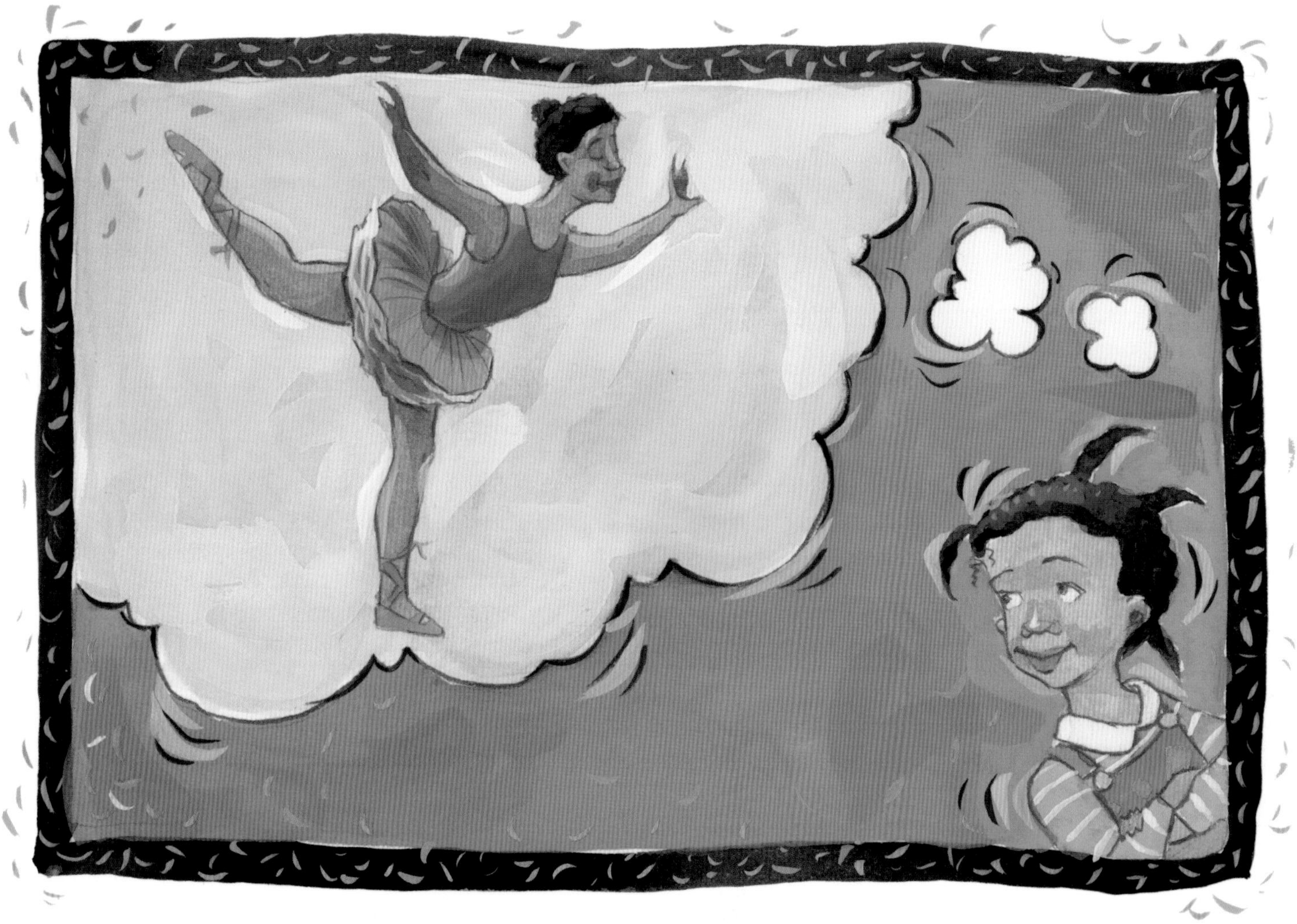

I can be a dancer.

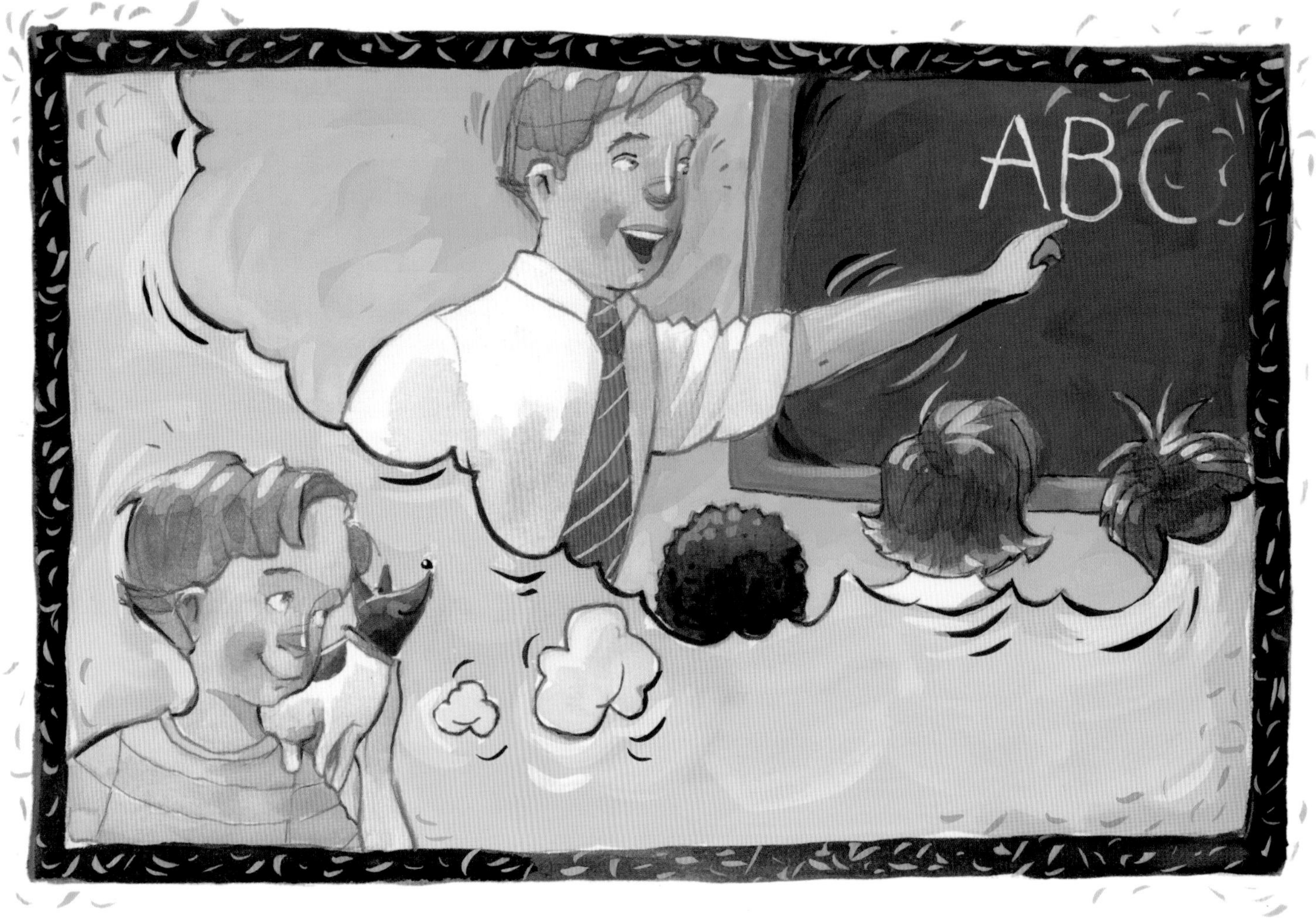

I can be a teacher.

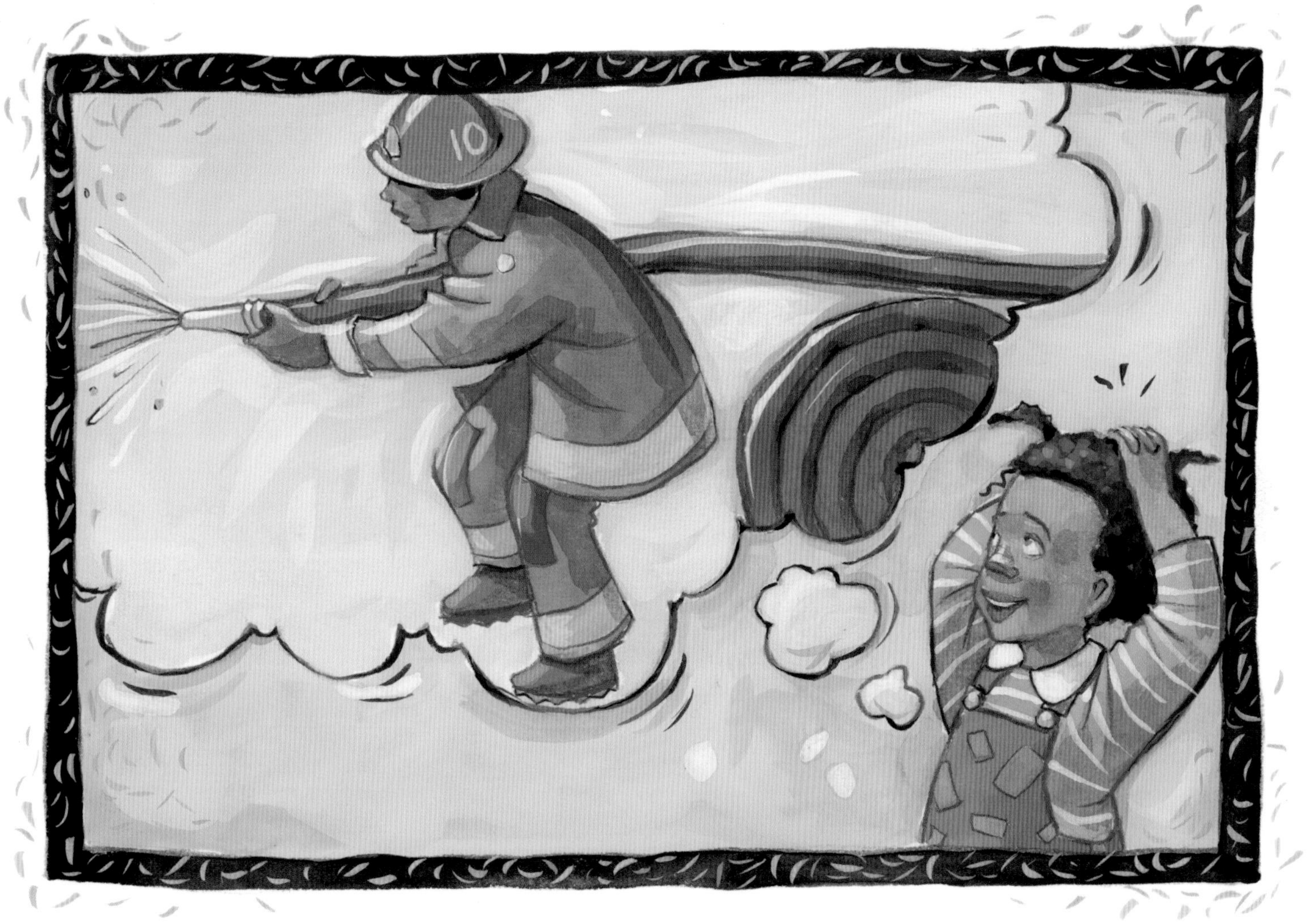

I can be a firefighter.

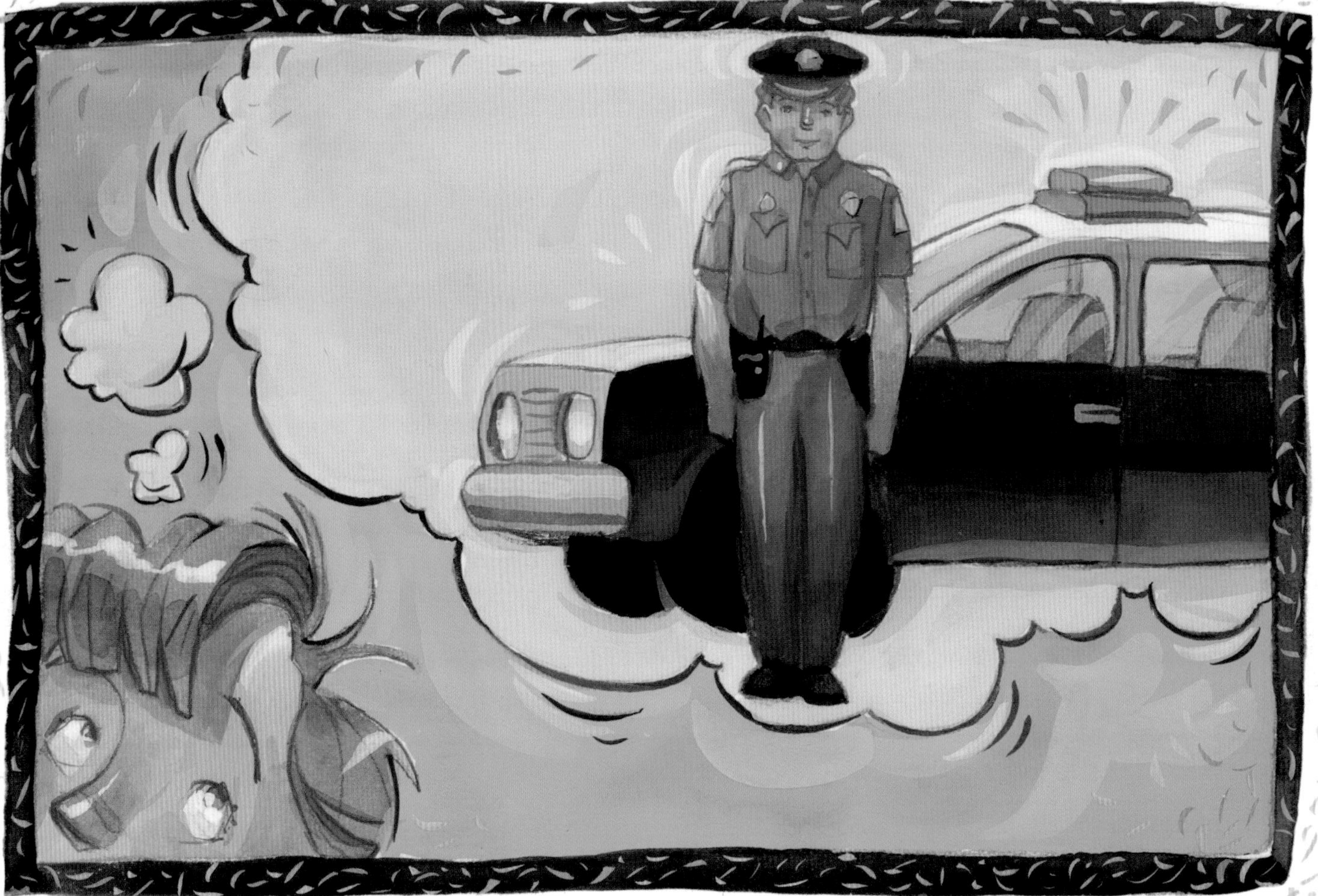

I can be a police officer.

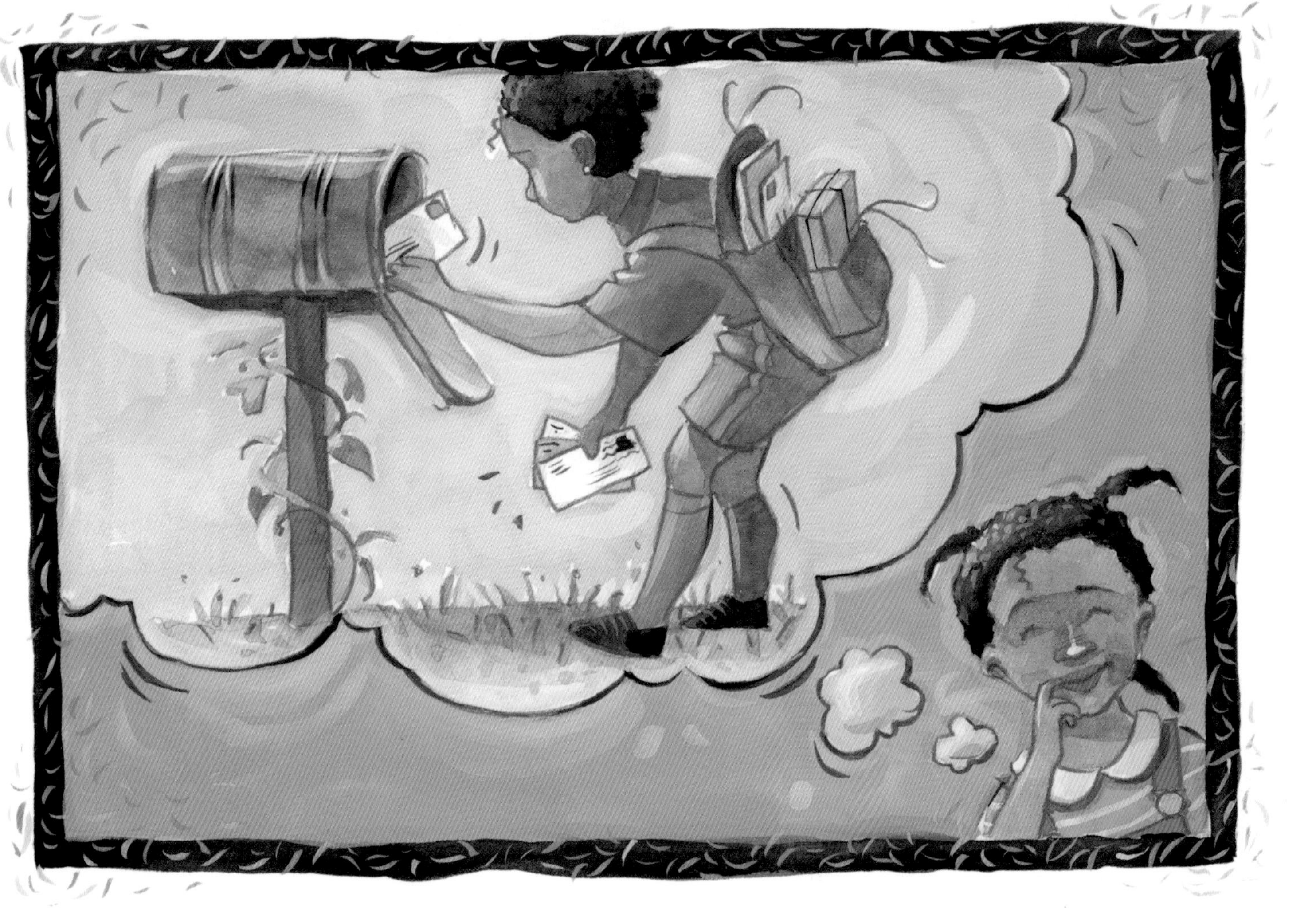

I can be a mail carrier.

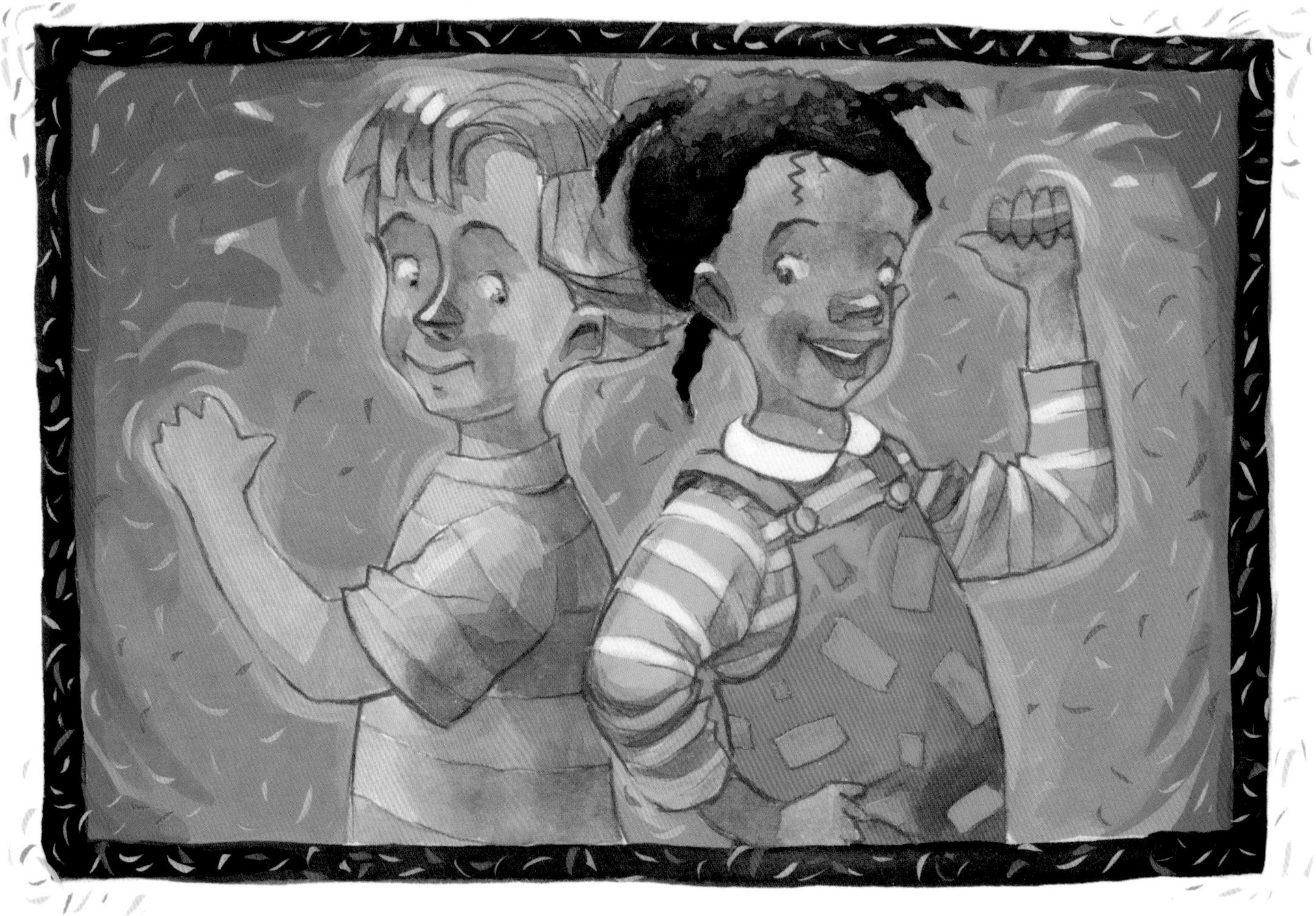

What can I be?
I can be me.